SPIRIT OF PLACE
PARIS

The last time I see Paris will be on the day I die. The city
was inexhaustible, and so is its memory.

ELLIOT PAUL, *THE LAST TIME I SAW PARIS*, 1942

Arcade Publishing
New York

THE WONDER OF PARIS

I cannot tell you what an immense impression Paris made upon me. It is the most extraordinary place in the World. I was not prepared for, and really could not have believed in, its perfectly direct and separate character. My eyes ached, and my head grew giddy, as novelty, novelty, novelty; nothing but strange and striking things; came swarming before me. I cannot conceive any place so perfectly and wonderfully expressive of its own character; its secret character no less than that which is on its surface; as Paris is. I walked about streets – in and out, up and down, backwards and forwards – during the two days we were there; and almost every house, and every person I passed, seemed to be another leaf in the enormous book that stands wide open there. I was perpetually turning over, and never coming nearer the end. There never was such a place for a description.

CHARLES DICKENS, LETTER TO COUNT D'ORSAY, 7 AUGUST 1844

Paris more than ever strikes me as the handsomest city in the world. I find nothing comparable to the view up and down the river, or to the liveliness of its streets. At night the river with its reflected lights, its tiny *bateaux mouches* with their ferret eyes, creeping stealthily along as if in search of prey, and the dimly outlined masses of building that wall it in, gives me endless pleasure.

JAMES RUSSELL LOWELL, 1819-91

A VIEW OF PARIS

I then came out and surveyed Paris from the front [of Sacré Coeur]. I could distinguish most of the landmarks – Notre Dame, Panthéon, Invalides, Gare d'Orleans, St Sulpice, and Louvre. Never before had I such a just idea of the immense size of the Louvre. I could also see the Opéra, (that centre of *Paris qui s'amuse*) with its green roof (? copper). And it looked so small and square and ordinary. And I thought of the world-famed boulevards and resorts lying hidden round about there. And I thought: Is that all it is? For a moment it seemed impossible to me that, as a result of a series of complicated conventions merely, that collocation of stones, etc (paving stones and building stones) could really be what it is – a synonym and symbol for all that is luxurious, frivolous, gay, vicious and artistic. I thought: 'Really, Paris is not Paris after all; it is only a collocation of stones.' The idea, though obvious enough, was very striking for a minute or two.

ARNOLD BENNETT, *JOURNAL*, 4 OCTOBER 1903

'THE ART OF LIVING . . .'

The French have always flattered themselves that they have gone further in the art of living, in what they call *l'entente de la vie*, than any other people, and with certain restrictions the claim is just. So far as man lives in his senses and his tastes he certainly lives as well here as he can imagine doing; and so far as he lives by the short run, as it were, rather than the long, he is equally well off. They seem to me to understand the 'long run' much better in England. There, if you live by the year, or by the semi-decade, say, you are free to find yourself at all points in relation with the world's best things. But the merit of Paris is that you have not to look so far ahead, and that without heavy machinery, by the day, by the month, by the season, you are surprisingly comfortable. There is to be found here, in other words, a greater amount of current well-being than elsewhere.

HENRY JAMES, LETTER TO *NEW YORK TRIBUNE*, 11 DECEMBER 1875

Paris, where you can get a sight of it, is really fine. The view from the bridges is even more imposing and picturesque than ours, though the bridges themselves and the river are not to compare with the Thames, or with the bridges that cross it. The mass of public buildings and houses, as seen from the Pont Neuf, rises up around you on either hand, whether you look up or down the river, in huge, aspiring, tortuous ridges, and produces a solidity of expression and a fantastic confusion not easy to reconcile. The clearness of the air, the glittering sunshine, and the cool shadows add to the enchantment of the scene. In bright day, it dazzles the eye like a steel mirror. . . Paris is a splendid vision, a fabric dug out of the earth and hanging over it. The stately, old-fashioned shops and jutting angles of the houses give it the venerable appearance of antiquity, while their texture and colour clothe it in a robe of modern splendour. It looks like a collection of palaces, or of ruins!

WILLIAM HAZLITT, *NOTES OF A JOURNEY THROUGH FRANCE AND ITALY*, 1826

The Eiffel Tower

This evening I dined on the platform of the Eiffel Tower with the Charpentiers, the Hermants, the Dayots, the Zolas, etc. Going up in the lift, I had a feeling in the pit of my stomach as if I were on a ship at sea, but no dizziness. Up there, we were afforded a realization, beyond anything imaginable at ground level, of the greatness, the extent, the Babylonian intensity of Paris, with odd buildings glowing in the light of the setting sun with the colour of Roman stone, and among the calm, sweeping lines of the horizon the steep, jagged silhouette of Montmartre looking in the dusky sky like an illuminated ruin. . .

A peculiar sensation, rather like taking a header into space, the sensation of coming down those open-work steps in the darkness, plunging every now and then into an infinite void, and one feels like an ant coming down the rigging of a man-of-war, rigging which has turned to iron.

EDMOND DE GONCOURT, *JOURNAL*, 2 JULY 1889

The merit of the Eiffel Tower is that he shows you not only Paris to the ultimate edges in every direction save on the northern slopes of Montmartre, but he shows you (almost) France too. How long the Eiffel Tower is to stand I cannot say, but I for one shall feel sorry and bereft when he ceases to straddle over Paris. For though he is vulgar he is great, and he has come to be a symbol. When he goes he will make a strange rent in the sky.

E. V. LUCAS, *A WANDERER IN PARIS*, 1909

Raoul Dufy

THE BOULEVARD SEBASTOPOL

It was the hour when passers-by no longer pause before shop windows. Night, with other aims in view, had come to life. There were lanterns on the carriages: the cabs with bright lights shining like two pleasure-hungry eyes, and the trams with red or green beacons roaring like an impatient crowd. They followed one another, crossed, stamped the ground and rolled on. On the horizon, in the direction of the Grands Boulevards, the light was far brighter and rose into the sky as though drawn by some luminous power. At this hour, the Boulevard Sébastopol, with its closed shops was no longer the goal. Cabs rushed by. Those bound for the Grands Boulevards went towards the light, hastening there like people attracted by a show.

The whole of the Boulevard Sébastopol lives on the pavement. On this broad area, in the blue air of a summer night, the day after the 14th July, Paris sifts and trails the residue of the holiday. The arc-lights, the trees' foliage, the moving vehicles, the diverse excitement of the passers-by, create something dense and sharp, an atmosphere both alcoholic and tired. A nightly spectacle, and yet many a façade and street corner retains a reminder of the day before. Certain noises, certain cries, recall the songs of last night's revellers. A few flags and lanterns hang at windows and seem to clamour for a renewal of festivities. One can guess what is taking place in people's minds. Those who enjoyed themselves yesterday are on the alert for some new delight. This is because men who have once known pleasure seek it eternally. While the others, those who are poor, those who are ugly, and those who are shy, make their way through the remains of the holiday and nose in the corners for some debris of pleasure that has been overlooked. This is because men who have never known pleasure are in torment and seek for it day after day until they grow weary of never having had anything at all.

CHARLES-LOUIS PHILIPPE, *BUBU DE MONTPARNASSE*, 1901

LATE-NIGHT PARIS

Paris – in appearance anyway – is a mighty gay place at night. The sidewalks are crowded with the little tables of the coffee and liqueur drinkers. The music of a hundred orchestras bursts forth from the lighted windows. The air is soft with the fragrance of a June evening, tempered by the curling smoke of fifty thousand cigars. Through the noise and chatter of the crowd there sounds unending the wail of the motor horn.

The hours of Parisian gaiety are late. Ordinary dinner is eaten at about seven o'clock, but fashionable dinners begin at eight or eight-thirty. Theatres open at a quarter to nine and really begin at nine o'clock. Special features and acts – famous singers and vaudeville artists – are brought on at eleven o'clock so that dinner-party people may arrive in time to see them. The theatres come out at midnight. After that there are the night suppers, which flourish till two or half-past. But, if you wish, you can go between the theatre and supper to some such sidelong place as the Moulin Rouge or the Bal Tabarin, which reach the height of their supposed merriment at about one in the morning.

At about two or two-thirty the motors come whirling home, squawking louder than ever, with a speed limit of fifty miles an hour. Only the best of them can run faster than that. Quiet, conservative people in Paris like to get to bed at three o'clock; after all, what is the use of keeping late hours and ruining one's health and complexion? If you make it a strict rule to be in bed by three, you feel all the better for it in the long run – health better, nerves steadier, eyes clearer, and you're able to get up early – at half-past eleven – and feel fine.

Those who won't or don't go to bed at three wander about the town, eat a second supper in an all-night restaurant, circulate round with guides, and visit the slums of the Market, where gaunt-eyed wretches sleep in crowded alleys in the mephitic air of a summer night, and where the idle rich may feed their luxurious curiosity on the sufferings of the idle poor.

STEPHEN LEACOCK, *BEHIND THE BEYOND*, 1918

NOTRE-DAME AND THE SEINE

I walked over to Notre Dame along the quays, and was more than ever struck with the brilliant picturesqueness of Paris as, from any part opposite the Louvre, you look up and down the Seine. The huge towers of Notre Dame, rising with their blue-gray tone from the midst of the great mass round which the river divides, the great Arc de Triomphe answering them with equal majesty in the opposite distance, the splendid continuous line of the Louvre between, and over it all the charming coloring of Paris on certain days – the brightness, the pearly grays, the flicker of light, the good taste, as it were, of the atmosphere – all this is an entertainment which even custom does not stale.

HENRY JAMES, LETTER TO *NEW YORK TRIBUNE*, 22 JANUARY 1876

THE PONT NEUF

If a Parisian acquaintance asks after your health, and if you wish to inform him that you are as fit as a fiddle, and at the same time impress him with your knowledge of French colloquialisms, you will say that you are feeling as fine as the Pont Neuf – 'Je me porte comme le Pont Neuf'.

The seven miles of the Seine which flow through Paris are crossed by thirty-one bridges, but to the true Parisian there is only one bridge that counts even today – the Pont Neuf. . .

It is from the hucksters of the Pont Neuf that the 'bouquinistes', the bookstall men of the quais, are descended. Likewise the birdshops, the dealers in dogs, rabbits, guinea pigs and such small animals, and the fishing tackle men, all had their beginning on the Pont Neuf. It must have been a joyous hurly-burly of humanity, that old Pont Neuf. Even now one feels, or imagines, that something of that old warm, noisy life still clings about it, and, at all events, among bridges it seems companionable compared to the others, perhaps because they are cold-blooded steel, and it still preserves its warm old stone.

RICHARD LE GALLIENNE, *FROM A PARIS GARRET*, 1943

Of all the bridges which were ever built, the whole world who have passed over the Pont Neuf must own that it is the noblest,—the finest,—the grandest,—the lightest,—the longest,—the broadest that ever conjoined land and land together upon the face of the terraqueous globe.

LAURENCE STERNE, *A SENTIMENTAL JOURNEY*, 1768

'PARIS AFTERNOONS'

Paris afternoons: Book-stalls along the quais, with old prints that nobody wants, naughty novels corseted in cellophane; animal shops on the Quai de Gesvres; ferrets, squirming and clucking in the straw, with red eyes and little yawns which reveal their fine white teeth; marmosets chattering over their stump of rotten banana, moulting parrots; the mysterious nocturnal creature that one is always tempted to buy – 'c'est un binturong, monsieur' – and then the walk back over the bridges; poplar trees eddying in the yellow river; misty black-and-grey streets of the Left Bank; discreet shops full of *bibelots*, bad modern paintings, Empire clocks.

Disorder of the hotel bedroom; books, paintings, clothes and red plush; shadows lengthening, the desirable afternoon sleep with its bewildering nightmare-starts and awakenings, its flash-backs to the past. Then the purple Neon lights shining in at the window and the concierge on the telephone: 'Il y a quelqu'un en bas qui vous demande'. 'Voulez-vous lui dire de monter.'

CYRIL CONNOLLY, *THE UNQUIET GRAVE*, 1945

Victor Gilbert

A FASHIONABLE DRIVE

So here we are in the Avenue du Bois de Boulogne, at the head of the famous promenade, Jacob's Ladder, as it were, with angels ascending and descending going to the Bois or returning from the Bois – angels with yellow wigs, angels with raven black switches, angels who wear their hair in flat *bandeaux*, like the virgins in Perugino's pictures, angels whose heads suggest those of the dancing maidens of Tangara or the 'majas' that Goya loved to paint. With huge hats or minute toques, mere garlands of sweet flowers, with garments that seem like a foam of lace and frills emerging from beneath long mantles of silk, velvet and brocade, the angels lean back voluptuously in elegant carriages, and graciously accord to mortals the calm spectacle of their various beauty and of their perfect toilets. From the Avenue du Bois de Boulogne the throng of carriages leads us to the Avenue des Acacias, the drive which fashion has selected in preference to more sunny, open, and picturesque avenues. And there between the gnarled and fantastic trunks of the acacia-trees the carriages advance slowly and with difficulty up and down, dazzling the eye with the radiant beauty of the blondes and brunettes, of angels ascending and descending, the joy of men.

Mingled with the carriages of the angels are the carriages of mortals, the landaus of the noble faubourg, the victorias of the club-men and ambassadors, the parade vehicles of all those who are afflicted with momentary or stable wealth. On foot, too, may be seen the young bloods, the pseudo-worldlings, the *pannés*, their eye-glasses fixed, correct and stiff, lounging with weary air, cackling and uttering flute-like squeaks of admiration as they watch the horses and the women, and waft salutations that are never returned. The afternoon drive in the Bois brings together, to see and to be seen, all the notabilities of fashionable Paris, the celebrities of society and of the stage, of leisure, of talent, of glory and of scandal.

THEODORE CHILD, *IN PRAISE OF PARIS*, 1893

SUNSET OVER PARIS

They followed the embankment, under the plane-trees, seeing the past rise up at every step as the landscape opened out before them: the bridges, their arches cutting across the satin sheen of the river; the Cité covered with shadow, dominated by the yellowing towers of Notre-Dame; the great sweeping curve of the right bank, bathed in sunshine, leading to the dim silhouette of the Pavillon de Flore; the broad avenues, the buildings on either bank, and between them, the Seine, with all the lively activity of its laundry-boats, its baths, its barges. As in the past, the setting sun seemed to follow them along the riverside, rolling over the roofs of the distant houses, partially eclipsed for a moment by the dome of the Institut. It was a dazzling sunset, finer than they had ever seen, a slow descent through tiny clouds which gradually turned into a trellis of purple with molten gold pouring through every mesh. But out of the past they were calling to mind nothing reached them but an unconquerable melancholy, a feeling that it would always be just beyond their reach, that it would be impossible to live it again. The time-worn stones were cold and the ever-flowing stream beneath the bridges seemed to have carried away something of their selves, the charm of awakening desire, the thrill of hope and expectation. Now they were all in all to each other, they had forgone the simple happiness of feeling the warm pressure of their arms as they strolled quietly along, wrapped, as it were, in the all-enveloping life of the great city.

EMILE ZOLA, *L'Oeuvre*, 1886

PARIS IN THE SPRING

With the fishermen and the life on the river, the beautiful barges with their own life on board, the tugs with their smoke-stacks that folded back to pass under the bridges, the great elms on the stone banks of the river, the plane trees and in some places the poplars, I could never be lonely along the river. With so many trees in the city, you could see the spring coming each day until a night of warm wind would bring it suddenly one morning. Sometimes the heavy cold rains would beat it back so that it would seem that it would never come and that you were losing a season out of your life. This was the only truly sad time in Paris because it was unnatural. You expected to be sad in the fall. Part of you died each year when the leaves fell from the trees and their branches were bare against the wind and the cold, wintry light. But you knew there would always be spring, as you knew the river would flow again after it was frozen. When the cold rains kept on and killed the spring, it was as though a young person had died for no reason.

ERNEST HEMINGWAY, *A MOVEABLE FEAST*, 1950

'PARIS LOVES LOVERS'

Paris loves lovers,
　　For lovers it's heaven above.
Paris tells lovers,
"Love is supreme,
Wake up your dream
And make love!"
Only in Paris one discovers,
The urge to merge with the splurge of the spring.
Paris loves lovers,
For lovers know that
Love is
Ev'ry—
Thing.

COLE PORTER, 'PARIS LOVES LOVERS', 1954

THE BOULEVARD DES ITALIENS

On the Boulevard des Italiens . . . the movement always seems leisured, and the conditions inviting. By day and by night the urban landscape spread out before our eyes is curious and fascinating. In the foreground we have the types of Paris and the universe, the private carriages, the hackney victorias, the gigantic three-horse omnibuses, the broad sidewalks shaded with trees, lined with shops and cafés, and dotted at intervals with tasteful kiosks for the sale of newspapers and flowers. Between the soft perspective of trees, surmounted by the upper stories of the houses and the irregular silhouettes of the chimneys, the road runs straight ahead to the vanishing point, which is lost in a maze of trees and tall metallic columns that carry the electric lights. Everything and everybody seems calm, neat and orderly. . . . Here is the Café Riche, less famous than of old; the Café Anglais, less sumptuous than of old; the Maison Dorée, the resort of *gourmets* who are wealthy, if not critical; the Café Tortoni, where a few famous wits of the boulevard press are on view during the absinthe hour.

THEODORE CHILD, *IN PRAISE OF PARIS*, 1893

THE PLACE DE LA CONCORDE

I never cross the Place de la Concorde without thinking of the contrast between its spacious exhilarating gaiety and its tragic history. The noble simplicity of its proportions, the dignity of the tall old mansions of the Rue de Rivoli that frame it on the north side, and the aerial sweep of its vistas across the river to the dome of the Invalides, and along the leafy avenue of the Bois de Boulogne to the Arc de Triomphe, make a spectacle of light and air irresistibly gladdening.

The saddest heart must be momentarily uplifted as it crosses the Place de la Concorde. And the visitor overlooking it from his windows in the Hôtel Crillon can truthfully feel that here are expressed as in a symbol the immortal buoyancy and vigour of the French spirit, and the unclouded reach and clarity of the French mind.

RICHARD LE GALLIENNE, *FROM A PARIS GARRET*, 1943

Cafés form one of the specialities of Paris, and some of them should be visited by the stranger who desires to see Parisian life in all its phases. An hour or two may be pleasantly spent in sitting at one of the small tables with which the pavements on front of the cafés on the Boulevards are covered on summer evenings, and watching the passing throng. Chairs placed in unpleasant proximity to the gutter should, of course, be avoided. Most of the Parisian men spend their evenings at the cafés, where they partake of coffee, liqueurs and ices, meet their friends, read the newspapers, or play at cards or billiards. . . The best cafés may with propriety be visited by ladies, but those on the north side of the Boulevards Montmartre and des Italiens should be avoided, as the society there is far from select.

KARL BAEDEKER, *PARIS*, 1882

I sometimes go to breakfast at a café on the Boulevard, which I formerly used to frequent with considerable regularity. Coming back there the other day, I found exactly the same group of habitués at their tables . . . Adolphe or Edouard, in his long white apron and his large patent-leather slippers, has a perfect recollection of 'les habitudes de Monsieur'. He remembers the table you preferred, the wine you drank, the news-paper you read. He greets you with the friend-liest of smiles, and remarks that it is a long time since he has had the pleasure of seeing Monsieur.

HENRY JAMES, *PORTRAITS OF PLACES*, 1883

STREET TRADERS

It is a pleasant thing to walk along the Boulevards and see how men live in Paris. One man has live snakes crawling about him and sells soap and essences. Another sells books which lie upon the ground. Another under my window all day offers a gold chain. Half a dozen walk up and down with some dozen walking sticks under the arm. A little further, one sells cane tassels at 5 sous. Here sits Boots brandishing his brush at every dirty shoe. Then you pass several tubs of gold fish. Then a man sitting at his table cleaning gold and silver spoons with emery and haranguing the passengers on its virtues. Then a person who cuts profiles with scissors – 'Shall be happy to take yours, Sir'. Then a table of card puppets which are made to crawl then a hand organ . . . then a flower merchant. Then a bird shop with 20 parrots, 4 swans, hawks and nightingales. . . All these are the mere boutiques on the sidewalk, moved about from place to place as the sun or rain or the crowd may lead them.

RALPH WALDO EMERSON, JOURNALS, JULY 1833

STREET ENTERTAINMENTS

The Boulevards have long since lost their old order and decorum; they are now filled with street performances of all kinds and descriptions. Music upon every instrument that can make it; fortune-tellers, conjurors, gymnasts, dancing dogs, mountebanks – every conceivable dance, trick, or sleight-of-hand for entrapping money.

NATHAN SHEPPARD, *SHUT UP PARIS*, 1871

Clowns and lion-tamers exhibit themselves on high *trétaux*. Fortune-tellers pullulate. There is a smell of acetylene and of wild beasts. Dancers and dwarfs, fat ladies and living skeletons, and other freaks of Nature, display their deformities. On a moving rink erratic tubs collide to the accompaniment of female screams. Girls slide on slippery slopes from great heights. Young men indulge in gross liberties; gilded pigs turn endlessly; and aeroplanes fastened to a centre hurl themselves through the air. There are circuses and boxing-shows; there is the inevitable roulette and there are coconut-shies. It is all confusion and clamour, blatant, blaring, flaring – the fun of the fair!

SISLEY HUDDLESTON, *IN AND ABOUT PARIS*, 1927

PARIS BY NIGHT

So, step by step, you reach the Place de l'Opéra. It is here that Paris makes one of its grandest impressions. You have before you the façade of the Théâtre, enormous and bold, resplendent with colossal lamps between the elegant columns, before which open Rue Auber and Rue Halévy; to the right, the great furnace of the Boulevard des Italiens; to the left, the flaming Boulevard des Capucines, which stretches out between the two burning walls of the Boulevard Madeleine, and turning around, you see the three great diverging streets which dazzle you like so many luminous abysses; Rue de la Paix, all gleaming with gold and jewels, at the end of which the Colonne Vendôme rises against the starry sky; the Avenue de l'Opéra inundated with electric light; Rue Quatre Septembre shining with its thousand gas jets, and seven continuous lines of carriages issuing from the two Boulevards and five streets, crossing each other rapidly on the square, and a crowd coming and going under a shower of rosy and whitest light diffused from the great ground-glass globes, which produce the effect of wreaths and garlands of full moons, colouring the trees, high buildings and the multitude with the weird and mysterious reflections of the final scene in a fairy ballet. Here one experiences for the moment the sensations produced by Hasheesh. That mass of gleaming streets which lead to the Théâtre Français, to the Tuileries, to the Concorde and Champs-Elysées, each one of which brings you a voice of the great Paris festival, calling and attracting you on seven sides, like the stately entrances of seven enchanted palaces, and kindling in your brain and veins the madness of pleasure.

EDMONDO DE AMICUS, *STUDIES OF PARIS*, 1879

LES HALLES AT DAWN

At present the luminous dial of Saint-Eustace was paling as a
night-light does when surprised by the dawn. The gas-jets in the
wine-shops in the neighbouring streets went out one by one, like stars
extinguished by the brightness. And Florent gazed at the vast markets
now gradually emerging from the gloom, from the dreamland in which
he had beheld them, stretching out their ranges of open palaces.
Greenish-grey in hue, they looked more solid now, and even more
colossal with their prodigious masting of columns upholding an endless
expanse of roofs. . . And by degrees, as the fires of dawn rose higher and
higher at the far end of the Rue Rambuteau, the mass of vegetation grew
brighter and brighter, emerging more and more distinctly from the
bluey gloom that clung to the ground.

EMILE ZOLA, *LE VENTRE DE PARIS*, 1873

'A REPRESENTATIVE PARIS SLUM'

It was a very narrow street – a ravine of tall leprous houses, lurching towards one another in queer attitudes, as though they had all been frozen in the act of collapse. All the houses were hotels and packed to the tiles with lodgers, mostly Poles, Arabs and Italians. At the front of the hotels were tiny *bistros*, where you could be drunk for the equivalent of a shilling. On Saturday nights about a third of the male population of the quarter was drunk. There was fighting over women, and the Arab navvies who lived in the cheapest hotels used to conduct mysterious feuds, and fight them out with chairs and occasionally revolvers. At night the policemen would only come through the street two together. It was a fairly rackety place. And yet amid the noise and dirt lived the usual respectable French shopkeepers, bakers and laundresses and the like, keeping themselves to themselves and quietly piling up small fortunes. It was quite a representative Paris slum.

GEORGE ORWELL, *DOWN AND OUT IN PARIS AND LONDON*, 1933

The models – what stories are there! Every Monday morning from ten to twenty present themselves, male and female, for inspection in *puris naturabilis* before the critical gaze of the students of the different ateliers. One after another they mount the throne and assume such academic poses of their own choosing as they imagine will display their points to the best advantage. The students then vote upon them, for and against, by raising the hand. The massier, standing beside the model, announces the result, and, if the vote is favourable, enrols the model for a certain week to come.

There is intense rivalry among the models. Strange to say, most of the male models in the schools in Paris are from Italy, the southern part especially. As a rule they have very good figures. They begin posing at the age of five or six, and follow the business until old age retires them. Crowds of them are at the gate of the Beaux-Arts early on Monday mornings. In the voting, a child may be preferred to his seniors, and yet the rate of payment is the same – thirty francs a week.

W. C. MORROW, *BOHEMIAN PARIS*, 1899

The life of the young artist here is the easiest, merriest, dirtiest existence possible. He comes to Paris, notably at sixteen, from his province; his parents settle forty pounds a year on him, and pay his master; he establishes himself in the Pays Latin, or in the new quarter of Notre Dame de Lorette (which is peopled with painters); he arrives at his *atelier* at a tolerably early hour, and labours among a score of companions as merry and poor as himself. Each gentleman has his favourite tobacco-pipe; and the pictures are painted in the midst of a cloud of smoke, and a din of puns and choice French slang, and a roar of choruses, of which no one can form an idea who has not been present at such an assembly.

WILLIAM MAKEPEACE THACKERAY, *THE PARIS SKETCHBOOK*, 1840

MONTMARTRE

Just before the rue Norvins passes the Place Jean-Baptiste Clément (named in honour of the poet who secured immortality by a single song, 'Temps des Cerises') is the rue des Saules, which descends sharply the western side of the Butte. At the corner of the rue Saint-Vincent, beloved of lovers, is the Lapin à Gill, the cabaret which, till quite recently, was perhaps the most famous in all Paris. It is an old cottage, half-hidden by trees, like an emerald among the grey modern apartment houses. It was mercifully saved from the speculative builder's pick-axe by Aristide Bruant, the chansonnier of the Butte, who bought the property.

CHARLES DOUGLAS, *ARTIST QUARTER*, 1941

The Moulin Rouge in those days, with its illuminated sails turning slowly against the sky of the Place Blanche, and its entrance, more brilliantly lit than the rest of the boulevard, that always made me think of the open maw of a monster, was an immense ballroom, where every evening ordinary people came to dance. They were not ordinary in the sad, drab sense of the word. Thousands of office girls, salesgirls, little housemaids and young clerks from all over the city could, for a few francs, live in the illusion of luxury and high life for an evening. Nowhere else at that time could one find such an orgy of electric bulbs and projectors. Two orchestras played in turn and exactly at eleven, when the couples were getting tired of waltzing or charlestoning, the floor was suddenly invaded by the frenetic cancan dancers. . .

The Moulin Rouge era marks a milestone in time, in space, and in depth. Hundreds of ghosts stir in my memory and together form something alive which I find inexpressible in words. One would have to bring to life a whole neighbourhood, an entire epoch with its own music, its own fashions, in which not only the silhouette of women was different, but even the expression in their eyes, their smiles, yes, even the shape of their faces.

GEORGES SIMENON, *THE PATIENT*, 1963

RISQUÉ NIGHTLIFE

At the Bal Bullier one had to take more than a passing glance to tell the boys from the girls, for the Mimis and Fantines had often tucked up their hair and donned sailors' clothes or a tuxedo. Others went in scantier attire and were more distinguishable. There were feminine Méphistos, Spanish dancers, little brunettes as bullfighters, and blondes as Oriental favorites of the harem. When the ball was over, this motley crowd romped down to supper along the 'Boul Mich' in their fantastic clothes, and had *Marennes vertes* and cold champagne and beer and sandwiches in the hosteleries of the Quartier Latin.

FRANK BERKELEY SMITH, *HOW PARIS AMUSES ITSELF*, 1903

Just to note what the Bal des Quat'z Arts was in 1908. Calvocoressi went to this year's ball, being officially invited as a director of the Russian opera. He said that there were a large number of women there absolutely naked, and many men who wore nothing but a ceinture of bones which concealed nothing. Calvo said that on leaving at 4 a.m. he saw a naked woman calmly standing outside in the street, smoking a cigarette, surrounded by a crowd of about 200 people. He said that he had heard that afterwards a procession of nudites was formed and went down the Champs Elysées.

ARNOLD BENNETT, *JOURNAL*, 29 MAY 1908

'THE LAST TIME I SAW PARIS'

The last time I saw Paris,
Her heart was warm and gay,
I heard the laughter of her heart in ev'ry street café.
The last time I saw Paris,
Her trees were dressed for spring
And lovers walked beneath those trees
And birds found songs to sing.
I dodged the same old taxicabs that I
    had dodged for years;
The chorus of their squeaky horns was music
    to my ears.
The last time I saw Paris,
Her heart was warm and gay –
No matter how they change her, I'll remember her that way.

OSCAR HAMMERSTEIN II & JEROME KERN, 'THE LAST TIME I SAW PARIS'

When spring comes to Paris the humblest mortal alive
must feel that he dwells in paradise.

HENRY MILLER, *TROPIC OF CANCER*, 1934

ACKNOWLEDGEMENTS

PICTURE CREDITS

Front cover: *Notre-Dame*, Albert Goodwin (Chris Beetles Ltd)
Back cover: *Outside the Théâtre du Vaudeville*, Jean Beraud (Fine Art Photographic Library)
Frontispiece: *Vue de Notre-Dame*, Paul Signac (JPL Fine Arts)
3: *Aerial view of Paris*, Alain Chartier (Landscape Only)
5: *Ile de la Cité, Seine and Palais du Louvre*, Luigi Loir (Fine Art Society)
7: *Sunny Afternoon near the Arc de Triomphe*, Albert William Lefebre (Fine Art Photographic)
9: *Pont-Neuf*, Daniel Barbier (Image Bank)
11. *La Tour Eiffel*, Raoul Dufy (Galerie Louis Carré, Paris)
13: *A Young lady looking towards the Châtelet, across the Boulevard Sebastopol*, Charles Lereoy-Saint-Aubert (Fine Art Photographic)
15: *Maxim's Restaurant*, Barry Lewis (Network)
17: *Notre-Dame*, Albert Goodwin (Chris Beetles Ltd)
19: *Pont-Neuf, Paris*, Pierre Auguste Renoir (National Gallery of Art, Washington; Ailsa Mellon Bruce Collection)
21: *Marchands aux bords de las Seine*, Victor Gabriel Gilbert (Fine Art Photographic/Galerie George)
23: *Park scene*, Jean Beraud (Fine Art Photographic)
25: *Pont Alexandre III*, Daniel Barbier (Image Bank)
27: *Le Louvre*, Paul Signac (JPL Fine Arts)
29: *Two lovers, Place d'Italie*, Brassai, Paris
30: Detail from *A Parisian woman in the Place de la Concorde*, Jean Beraud (Bridgeman/Musée Carnavalet)
31: *Le Boulevard des Italiens*, Edmond-Georges Grandjean (Bridgeman Art Library)
33: *Place de la Concorde*, Gustave Fraipont (Fine Art Photographic/Gavin Graham Gallery)
34: *Café tiles*, Volker Hinz (Image Bank)
35: *La Pâtisserie Gloppe, Champs-Elysées*, Jean Beraud (Bridgeman Musée Carnavalet, Paris)
37: *La Marche à la Ferraille*, Carlos Buffin (Fine Art Photographic)
38, 39: *Paris street entertainers*, Barry Lewis (Network)
41: *Paris by Night*, Louis Besson (Fine Art Photographic/Cadogan Gallery)
43: *Les Halles*, B. Annebicque (Sygma/John Hillelson Agency)
45: *Parisian Street*, Victor Gabriel Gilbert (Sotheby's)
47: *L'Atelier*, Prosper Louis Vagnier (Whitford & Hughes Ltd)
49: *Montmartre*, Robert Dowling
50: *High-Steppers*, Walter Sickert (Bridgeman/Mayor Gallery)
51: *Bal Moulin Rouge*, Anon. (Hulton Picture Library)
53: *Opening of the Tabarin Ball*, Anon. (Sotheby's)
55: *Paris in the spring*, John Sims

TEXT CREDITS

Text extracts from the following sources are reprinted with the kind permission of the publishers and copyright holders stated. Should any copyright holder have been inadvertently omitted they should apply to the publishers who will be pleased to credit them in full in any subsequent editions.

14: Stephen Leacock, *Behind the Beyond* (Bodley Head, 1918; the Estate of Stephen Leacock); 20: Cyril Connolly, *The Unquiet Grave* (Hamish Hamilton, 1945, reprinted by permission of Rogers, Coleridge & White); 26: Ernest Hemingway, *A Moveable Feast* (Jonathan Cape, 1950; reprinted by permission of the Executors of the Ernest Hemingway Estate); 28: Cole Porter, 'Paris Loves Lovers', Buxton-Hill Music Corp / Chappell Music Ltd; 44: George Orwell, *Down and Out in Paris and London* (Victor Gollancz, 1933, reprinted by permission of the Estate of the late Sonia Brownell Orwell and Secker & Warburg Ltd and Harcourt Brace Jovanovich, Inc.); 48: Charles Douglas, *Artist Quarter* (Faber & Faber, 1941); 50: George Simenon, *The Patient* (Hamish Hamilton, 1963); 54: Oscar Hammerstein II & Jerome Kern, 'The Last Time I Saw Paris' (T.B. Harms, Inc. / Chappell Music Ltd).

First U.S. Edition

Library of Congress Cataloguing-in-Publication Data is available.

ISBN 1-55970-009-2

Published in the United States by Arcade Publishing, Inc., New York,
a Little, Brown company.

10   9   8   7   6   5   4   3   2   1

Conceived, edited and designed by Russell Ash and Bernard Higton
Printed in Spain by Cayfosa, Barcelona